The Nativity & Early Life of St. John the Forerunner

Written by Lily Parascheva Rowe
Illustrated by Roland J. Ford

St. Stylianos Books
www.stylianosbooks.com
Copyright © 2012 St. Stylianos Books
1442 Dartmouth Avenue, Parkville, MD 21234
ISBN: 978-0-9831531-6-0

Second Edition

Troparion of the Nativity of St. John the Forerunner:

"O Prophet and Forerunner of the coming of Christ, we honour thee lovingly but cannot extol thee worthily; for by thy birth thy mother's barrenness and thy father's dumbness were unloosed, and the Incarnation of the Son of God is proclaimed to the world."

Kontakion of the Nativity of St. John the Forerunner:

"The formerly barren one today gives birth to the Forerunner of Christ Who is the fulfillment of prophecy. For the Prophet, Herald and Forerunner of the Word submitted to Him Whom the prophets foretold by laying his hand on Him in the Jordan."

This is the icon of the Feast of the Nativity of St. John the Forerunner. We celebrate this feast on June 24th [July 7th]. We also commemorate St. John every Tuesday.

Zachariah and Elizabeth were very faithful to God. They wanted children, but were too old to have them.

Zachariah was a High Priest of the Temple. He burned incense at the altar, leading the people in prayer.

An angel greeted him and said, "Do not be afraid, Zacharias, for your prayer is heard; and your wife Elizabeth will bear you a son, and you shall call his name John. And you will have joy and gladness, and many will rejoice at his birth. For he will be great in the sight of the Lord, and shall drink neither wine nor strong drink." Luke 1:13-14

"He will also be filled with the Holy Spirit, even from his mother's womb. And he will turn many of the children of Israel to the Lord their God. He will also go before Him in the spirit and power of Elijah, 'to turn the hearts of the fathers to the children,' and the disobedient to the wisdom of the just, to make ready a people prepared for the Lord." Luke 1:15-17

Zachariah did not believe him. The angel told Zachariah that because he did not believe, he would be unable to speak until everything the angel said had taken place.

Zachariah stayed in the Holy Place for a long time. When he came out he could not speak, so people thought he had seen a vision. After he had finished with his duties as a priest, he returned home.

Elizabeth was soon pregnant, even though she was very old. This made them very happy. They thanked God for blessing them.

Mary, Elizabeth's relative, went to visit her. The Theotokos was also going to have a baby. When Elizabeth heard Mary's voice, the baby inside her leapt for joy. Elizabeth said to Mary, "Blessed are you among women, and blessed is the fruit of your womb!"

Elizabeth gave birth to a son. When the baby was eight days old, the priest came to circumcise him and give him a name. Elizabeth said that his name was John. Since he could not speak, Zechariah wrote, "His name is John." Many people heard about John and his miraculas birth.

Zachariah's voice returned to him and he could speak again. He was filled with the Holy Spirit and prophesied. He gave glory to God for John who would be the Forerunner of Christ.

King Herod was not pleased to hear about John's birth. Herod thought John might be the new king, which the wisemen told him about. The evil king hoped to destroy Christ. Herod ordered all the male children under age two years old to be destroyed. Zachariah was also martyred while serving in the Temple because he would not tell the soldiers where John and Elizabeth were hiding.

When Elizabeth heard that King Herod was searching for John, she took John and fled into the wilderness.

A mountain opened to reveal a secret cave. Elizabeth and John hid themselves inside. The soldiers looked everywhere for them, but did not find them.

Joseph had a dream in which God told him to take Jesus and the Theotokos to Egypt. Joseph obeyed God's command and the family was kept safe from evil King Herod.

The soldiers were not able to find Christ. Both John and Our Lord Jesus were safely hidden. They were protected by God, just as Moses had been safely hidden in the basket a long time ago.

John was still young when Elizabeth fell asleep in the Lord. God looked after John in the wilderness, just as He had looked after the Isrealites. When he grew up, John baptized people for the forgiveness of their sins.

Dear Parents,

This book tells the story of the Nativity & Early Life of St. John the Forerunner, as celebrated in the Orthodox Church. Through repetition, your child will learn to recognize the icon depicting his birth, and understand the elements within the icon. It is our hope that this book, and others produced by St. Stylianos Books, will be tools useful to parents who are educating their children in the Orthodox Faith.

Our books are intended to be a teaching aid for children at various stages of development. When enjoying them with toddlers, simply identify the people in the pictures. For preschool aged children, simplify the narration by omitting the longer hymns. By five years of age, children should be able to listen to an entire story.

We hope that our books will inspire children to learn about the saints of the Church and will remain stimulating for many years to come. We thank you for your support.

Blessings,
St. Stylianos Books

St. Stylianos Books
Orthodox Children's Books
www.StylianosBooks.com

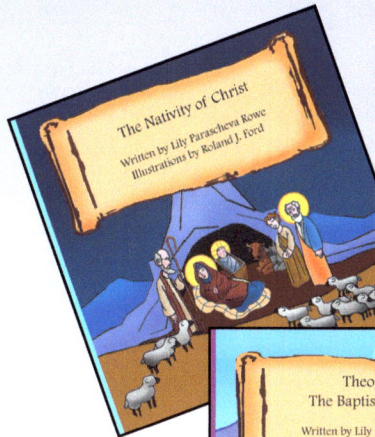

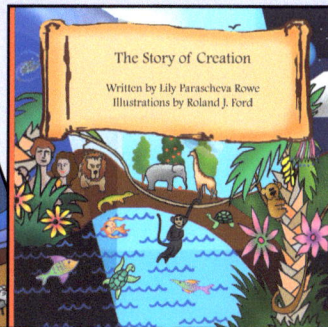

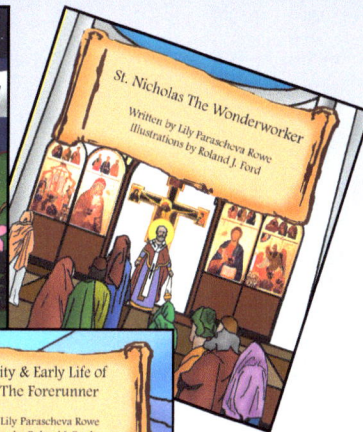

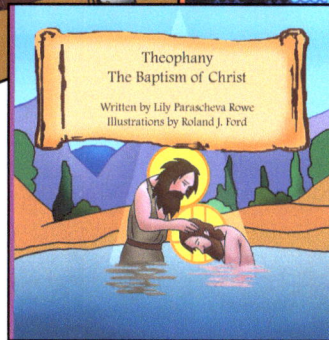

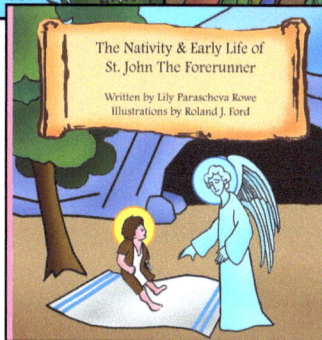

The Nativity of Christ
Written by Lily Parascheva Rowe
Illustrations by Roland J. Ford

The Story of Creation
Written by Lily Parascheva Rowe
Illustrations by Roland J. Ford

St. Nicholas The Wonderworker
Written by Lily Parascheva Rowe
Illustrations by Roland J. Ford

Theophany
The Baptism of Christ
Written by Lily Parascheva Rowe
Illustrations by Roland J. Ford

The Nativity & Early Life of
St. John The Forerunner
Written by Lily Parascheva Rowe
Illustrations by Roland J. Ford

www.ingramcontent.com/pod-product-compliance
Lightning Source LLC
Chambersburg PA
CBHW042113040426
42448CB00002B/259